Adobe InDesign
Keyboard Shortcuts

By

U. C-Abel Books.

All Rights Reserved

First Edition: 2017

ISBN-13: 978-1543228120
ISBN-10: 1543228127.

Published by U. C-Abel Books.

Table of Contents

Acknowledgement.

All thanks to God Almighty for enabling us to bring this work to this point. He is a wonder indeed.

We want to specially appreciate the great company, Adobe Systems Inc. for their hard work and style of reasoning in providing the public with helpful programs and resources, and for helping us with some of the tips and keyboard shortcuts included in this book.

Dedication

The dedication of this title goes to every user of Adobe InDesign.

How We Began.

We enjoy using shortcuts because they set us on a high plane that astonishes people around us when we work with them. As wonderful shortcuts users, the worst eyesore we witness in computer operation is to see somebody sluggishly struggling to execute a task through mouse usage when in actual sense shortcuts will help to save that person time. Most people have asked us to help them with a list of keyboard shortcuts that can make them work as smartly as we do and that drove us into research to broaden our knowledge and truly help them as they demanded, that is the reason for the existence of this book. It is a great tool for lovers of shortcuts, and those who want to join the group.

Most times the things we love don't come by easily. It is our love for keyboard shortcuts that made us to bear long sleepless nights like owls just to make sure we get the best out of it, and it is the best we got that we are sharing with you in this book. You cannot be the same at computing after reading this book. The time you entrusted to our care is an expensive possession and we promise not to mess it up.

Thank you.

What to Know Before You Begin.

General Notes.

1. Most of the keyboard shortcuts you will see in this book refer to the U.S. keyboard layout. Keys for other layouts might not correspond exactly to the keys on a U.S. keyboard. Keyboard shortcuts for laptop computers might also differ.

2. It is important to note that when using shortcuts to perform any command, you should make sure the target area is active, if not, you may get a wrong result. Example, if you want to highlight all texts you must make sure the text field is active and if an object, make sure the object area is active. The active area is always known by the location where the cursor of your computer blinks.

3. On a Mac keyboard, the Command key is denoted with the ⌘symbol.

4. If a function key doesn't work on your Mac as you expect it to, press the Fn key in addition to the function key. If you don't want to press the Fn key every time, you can change your Apple system preferences.

5. The plus (+) sign that comes in the middle of keyboard shortcuts simply means the keys are

meant to be combined or held down together not to be added as one of the shortcut keys. In a case where plus sign is needed; it will be duplicated (++).

6. Many keyboards assign special functions to function keys, by default. To use the function key for other purposes, you have to press Fn+the function key.

7. For keyboard shortcuts in which you press one key immediately followed by another key, the keys are separated by a comma (,).

8. It is also important to note that the keyboard shortcuts, tips, and techniques listed in this book are for users of Adobe InDesign.

9. To get more information on this title visit ucabelbooks.wordpress.com and search the site using keywords related to it.

10. Our chief website is under construction.

Some Short Forms You Will Find in This Book and Their Full Meaning.

Here are short forms used in this Adobe InDesign Keyboard Shortcuts book and their full meaning.

1.	Win	-	Windows logo key
2.	Tab	-	Tabulate Key
3.	Shft	-	Shift Key
4.	Prt sc	-	Print Screen
5.	Num Lock	-	Number Lock Key
6.	F	-	Function Key
7.	Esc	-	Escape Key
8.	Ctrl	-	Control Key
9.	Caps Lock	-	Caps Lock Key
10.	Alt	-	Alternate Key

CHAPTER 1.

Fundamental Knowledge of Keyboard Shortcuts.

Without the existence of the keyboard, there wouldn't have been anything like keyboard shortcuts so in this chapter we will learn a little about the computer keyboard before moving to keyboard shortcuts.

1. Definition of Computer Keyboard.

This is an input device that is used to send data to computer memory.

Sketch of a Keyboard

1.1 Types of Keyboard.

i. Standard (Basic) Keyboard.
ii. Enhanced (Extended) Keyboard.

i. **Standard Keyboard:** This is a keyboard designed during the 1800s for mechanical typewriters with just 10 function keys (F keys) placed at the left side of it.

ii. **Enhanced Keyboard:** This is the current 101 to 102-key keyboard that is included in almost all the personal computers (PCs) of nowadays, which has 12 function keys, usually at the top side of it.

Function Keys

Numeric Keys

Alphabetic keys

1.2 Segments of the keyboard

- Numeric keys.
- Alphabetic keys.
- Punctuation keys.
- Windows Logo key.
- Function keys.
- Special keys.

Numeric Keys: Numeric keys are keys with numbers from **0 - 9**.

Alphabetic Keys: These are keys that have alphabets on them, ranging from **A** to **Z**.

Punctuation Keys: These are keys of the keyboard used for punctuation, examples include comma, full stop, colon, question marks, hyphen, etc.

Windows Logo Key: A key on Microsoft Computer keyboard with its logo displayed on it. Search for this ⊞ on your keyboard.

Apple Key: This also known as Command key is a modifier key that you can find on an Apple keyboard. It usually has the image of an apple or command logo on it. Search for this on your Apple keyboard ⌘

Function Keys: These are keys that have **F** on them which are usually combined with other keys. They are F1 - F12, and are also in the class called *Special Keys*.

Special Keys: These are keys that perform special functions. They include: Tab, Ctrl, Caps lock, Insert, Prt sc, alt gr, Shift, Home, Num lock, Esc, and many others. Special keys differ according to the type of computer involved. In some keyboard layout, especially laptops, the keys that turn the speaker on/off, the one that increases/decreases volume, the key that turns the computer Wifi on/off are also special keys.

Other Special Keys Worthy of Note.

Enter Key: This is located at the right-hand corner of most keyboards. It is used to send messages to the computer to execute commands, in most cases it is used to mean "Ok" or "Go".

Escape Key (ESC): This is the first key on the upper left of most keyboards. It is used to cancel routines, close menus and select options such as **Save** according to circumstances.

Control Key (CTRL): It is located on the bottom row of the left and right hand side of the keyboard. They also work with the function keys to execute commands using Keyboard shortcuts (key combinations).

Alternate Key (ALT): It is located on the bottom row also of some keyboard, very close to the CTRL key on both side of the keyboard. It enables many editing functions to be accomplished by using some keystroke combinations on the keyboard.

Shift Key: This adds to the roles of function keys. In addition, it enables the use of alternative function of a particular button (key), especially, those with more than one function on a key. E.g. use of capital letters, symbols, and numbers.

1.3. Selecting/Highlighting With Keyboard.

This is a highlighting method or style where data is selected using the computer keyboard instead of a computer mouse.

To do this:

- Move your cursor to the text or object you want to highlight, make sure that area is active,
- Hold down the shift key with one finger,
- Then use another finger to move the arrow key that points to the direction you want to highlight.

1.4 The Operating Modes Of The Keyboard.

Just like the computer mouse, keyboard has two operating modes. The two modes are Text Entering Mode and Command Mode.

a. **Text Entering Mode:** this mode gives the operator/user the opportunity to type text.
b. **Command Mode:** this is used to command the operating system/software/application to execute commands in certain ways.

2. Ways To Improve In Your Typing Skill.

1. Put Your Eyes Off The Keyboard.

This is the aspect of keyboard usage that many don't find funny because they always ask. "How can I put my eyes off the keyboard when I am running away from the occurrence of errors on my file?" My aim is to be fast, is this not going to slow me down?

Of course, there will be errors and at the same time your speed will slow down but the motive behind the introduction to this method is to make you faster than you are. Looking at your keyboard while you type can make you get a sore neck, it is better you learn to touch type because the more you type with your eyes fixed on the screen instead of the keyboard, the faster you become.

An alternative to keeping your eyes off your keyboard is to use the "*Das Keyboard Ultimate*".

2. Errors Challenge You

It is better to fail than to not try at all. Not trying at all is an attribute of the weak and lazybones. When you make mistakes, try again because errors are opportunities for improvement.

3. Good Posture (Position Yourself Well).

Do not adopt an awkward position while typing. You should get everything on your desk organized or arranged before sitting to type. Your posture while typing contributes to your speed and productivity.

4. Practice

Here is the conclusion of everything said above. You have to practice your shortcuts constantly. The practice alone is a way of improvement. "Practice brings improvement". Practice always.

2.1 Software That Will Help You Improve Your Typing Skill.

There are several Software programs for typing that both kids and adults can use for their typing skill. Here is a list of software that can help you improve in your typing: Mavis Beacon, Typing Instructor, Mucky Typing Adventure, Rapid Tying Tutor, Letter Chase Tying Tutor, Alice Touch Typing Tutor and many more. Personally, I love Mavis Beacon.

To learn typing using MAVIS BEACON, install Mavis Beacon software to your computer, start with keyboard lesson, then move to games. Games like **Penguin Crossing, Creature Lab**, or **Space Junk** will help you become a professional in typing. Typing and keyboard shortcuts work hand-in-hand.

Sketch of a computer mouse

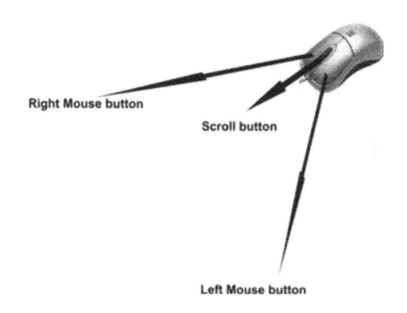

Right Mouse button

Scroll button

Left Mouse button

3. Mouse:

This is an oval-shaped portable input device with three buttons for scrolling, left clicking, and right clicking that enables work to be done effectively on a computer. The plural form of mouse is mice.

3.1 Types of Computer Mouse

- Mechanical Mouse.
- Optical Mechanical Mouse (Optomechanical).
- Laser Mouse.

- Optical Mouse.
- BlueTrack Mouse.

3.2 Forms of Clicking:

Left Clicking: This is the process of clicking the left side button of the mouse. It can also be called *clicking* without the addition of *left*.

Right Clicking: It is the process of clicking the right side button of a computer mouse.

Double Clicking: It is the process of clicking the left side button two times (twice) and immediately.

Triple Clicking: It is the process of clicking the left side button three times (thrice) and immediately.

Double clicking is used to select a word while triple clicking is used to select a sentence or paragraph.

Scroll Button: It is the little key attached to the mouse that looks like a tiny wheel. It takes you up and down a page when moved.

3.3 Mouse Pad: This is a small soft mat that is placed under the mouse to make it have a free movement.

3.4 Laptop Mouse Touchpad

This unlike the mouse we explained above is not external, rather it is inbuilt (comes with the laptop computer). With the presence of a laptop mouse touchpad, an external mouse is not needed to use a laptop, except in a case where it is malfunctioning or the operator prefers to use external one for some reasons.

The laptop mouse touchpad is usually positioned at the end of the keyboard section of a laptop computer. It is rectangular in shape with two buttons positioned below it. The two buttons/keys are used for left and right clicking just like the external mouse. Some laptops come with four mouse keys. Two placed above the mouse for left and right clicking and two other keys placed below it for the same function.

4. Definition Of Keyboard Shortcuts.

Keyboard shortcuts are defined as a series of keys, most times with combination that execute tasks which typically involve the use of mouse or other input devices.

5. Why You Should Use Shortcuts.

1. One may not be able to use a computer mouse easily because of disability or pain.

2. One may not be able to see the mouse pointer as a result of vision impairment, in such case what will the person do? The answer is SHORTCUT.

3. Research has made it known that Extensive mouse usage is related to Repetitive Syndrome Injury (RSI) greatly than the use of keyboard.

4. Keyboard shortcuts speed up computer users, making learning them a worthwhile effort.

5. When performing a job that requires precision, it is wise that you use the keyboard instead of mouse, for instance, if you are dealing with Text Editing, it is better you handle it using keyboard shortcuts than spending more time doing it with your computer mouse alone.

6. Studies calculate that using keyboard shortcuts allows working 10 times faster than working with the mouse. The time you spend looking for the mouse and then getting the cursor to the position you want is lost! Reducing your work duration by 10 times gives you greater results.

5.1 Ways To Become A Lover Of Shortcuts.

1. Always have the urge to learn new shortcut keys associated with the programs you use.
2. Be happy whenever you learn a new shortcut.

3. Try as much as you can to apply the new shortcuts you learnt.
4. Always bear it in mind that learning new shortcuts is worth it.
5. Always remember that the use of keyboard shortcuts keeps people healthy while performing computer activities.

5.2 How To Learn New Shortcut Keys
1. Do a research on them: quick references (a cheat sheet comprehensively compiled like ours) can go a long way to help you improve.
2. Buy applications that show you keyboard shortcuts every time you execute an action with mouse.
3. Disconnect your mouse if you must learn this fast.
4. Read user manuals and help topics (Whether offline or online).

5.3 Your Reward For Knowing Shortcut Keys.
1. You will get faster unimaginably.
2. Your level of efficiency will increase.
3. You will find it easy to use.
4. Opportunities are high that you will become an expert in what you do.
5. You won't have to go for **Office button**, click **New,** click **Blank and Recent**, and click **Create**

just to insert a fresh/blank page. **Ctrl +N** takes care of that in a second.

A Funny Note: Keyboarding and Mousing are in a marital union with Keyboarding being the head, so it will be unfair for anybody to put asunder between them.

5.4 Why We Emphasize On The Use of Shortcuts.

You may never leave your mouse completely unless you are ready to make your brain a box of keyboard shortcuts which will really be frustrating, just imagine yourself learning all shortcuts that go with the programs you use and their various versions. You shouldn't learn keyboard shortcuts that way.

Why we are emphasizing on the use of shortcuts is because mouse usage is becoming unusually common and unhealthy, too. So we just want to make sure both are combined so you can get fast, productive and healthy in your computer activities. All you need to know is just the most important ones associated with the programs you use.

CHAPTER 2.

15 (Fifteen) Special Keyboard Shortcuts.

The fifteen special keyboard shortcuts are fifteen (15) shortcuts every computer user should know.

The following is a list of keyboard shortcuts every computer user should know:

1. **Ctrl + A:** Control A, highlights or selects everything you have in the environment where you are working.

    *If you are like **"Wow, the content of this document is large and there is no time to select all of it, besides, it's going to mount pressure on my computer?"** Using the mouse for this is an outdated method of handling a task like selecting all, Ctrl+A will take care of that in a second.*

2. **Ctrl + C:** Control C copies any highlighted or selected element within the work environment.

    Saves the time and stress which would have been used to right click and click again just to copy. Use ctrl+c.

3. **Ctrl + N:** Control N opens a new window or file.

    Instead of clicking **File, New, blank/ template** *and another* **click,** *just press* **Ctrl + N** *and a fresh page or window will appear instantly.*

4. **Ctrl + O:** Control O opens a new program.

    Use ctrl +O when you want to locate / open a file or program.

5. **Ctrl + P:** Control P prints the active document.

    Always use this to locate the printer dialog box, and thereafter print.

6. **Ctrl + S:** Control S saves a new document or file and changes made by the user.

    Please stop! Don't use the mouse. Just press Ctrl+S and everything will be saved.

7. **Ctrl +V:** Control V pastes copied elements into the active area of the program in use.

Using ctrl+V in a case like this Saves the time and stress of right clicking and clicking again just to paste.

8. **Ctrl + W:** Control W is used to close the page you are working on when you want to leave the work environment.

    "There is a way Debby does this without using the mouse. Oh my God, why didn't I learn it then?" Don't worry, I have the answer. Debby presses Ctrl+W to close active windows.

9. **Ctrl + X:** Control X cuts elements (making the elements to disappear from their original place). The difference between cutting and deleting elements is that in Cutting, what was cut doesn't get lost permanently but prepares itself so that it can be pasted on another location defined by the user.

    *Use ctrl+x when you think **"this shouldn't be here and I can't stand the stress of retyping or redesigning it on the rightful place it belongs".***

10. **Ctrl + Y:** Control Y undoes already done actions.

    Ctrl+Z brought back what you didn't need? Press Ctrl+ Y to remove it again.

11. **Ctrl + Z:** Control Z redoes actions.
    Can't find what you typed now or a picture you inserted, it suddenly disappeared or you mistakenly removed it? Press Ctrl+Z to bring it back.

12. **Alt + F4:** Alternative F4 closes active windows or items.

    *You don't need to move the mouse in order to close an active window, just press **Alt + F4**. Also use it when you are done or you don't want somebody who is coming to see what you are doing.*

13. **Ctrl + F6:** Control F6 Navigates between open windows, making it possible for a user to see what is happening in windows that are active.
    Are you working in Microsoft Word and want to find out if the other active window where your browser is loading a page is still progressing? Use Ctrl + F6.

14. **F1:** This displays the help window.

    *Is your computer malfunctioning? Use **F1** to find help when you don't know what next to do.*

15. **F12:** This enables user to make changes to an already saved document.

> *F12 is the shortcut to use when you want to change the format in which you saved your existing document, password it, change its name, change the file location or destination, or make other changes to it. It will save you time.*

Note: The Control (Ctrl) key on Windows and Linux operating system is the same thing as Command (Cmmd) key on a Macintosh computer. So if you replace Control with Command key on a Mac computer for the special shortcuts listed above, you will get the same result.

CHAPTER 3.

Keyboard Shortcuts for use in InDesign.

About the application: It is a desktop publishing application developed by Adobe Systems. It helps in the production of flyers, brochures, posters, magazines, newspapers, and books.

A fresh topic ⌐↳

Default keyboard shortcuts in Adobe InDesign.

Adobe InDesign provides shortcuts to help you quickly work in documents without using the mouse. Many keyboard shortcuts appear next to the command names in menus. You can use the default InDesign shortcut set, the QuarkXPress 4.0 or Adobe PageMaker 7.0 shortcut set, or a shortcut set that you create. You can share shortcut sets with others using InDesign on the same platform.

InDesign provides shortcuts to help you quickly work in documents without using the mouse. Many keyboard shortcuts appear next to the command names in menus. You can use the default InDesign shortcut set or a shortcut set that you create. You can share shortcut sets with others using InDesign on the same platform.

Keys for Tools .

Note:

This table isn't a complete list of keyboard shortcuts. It lists only those shortcuts that aren't displayed in menu commands or tool tips.

Note:

Choose Window > Utilities > Tool Hints, and then select a tool to view its shortcuts and modifier keys.

Use the following list of keyboard shortcuts to enhance your productivity in Adobe InDesign.

Tool	Windows Shortcut	Mac OS Shortcut
Selection tool	V, Esc	V, Esc
Direct Selection tool	A	A

Toggle Selection and Direct Selection tool	Ctrl+Tab	Command+Control+Tab
Page tool	Shift+P	Shift+P
Gap tool	U	U
Pen tool	P	P
Add Anchor Point tool	=	=
Add Anchor Point tool	=	= (on the numeric pad)
Delete Anchor Point tool	-	-
Delete Anchor Point tool		-
Convert Direction Point tool	Shift+C	Shift+C
Type tool	T	T
Type On A Path tool	Shift+T	Shift+T
Pencil tool (Note tool)	N	N
Line tool	\	\
Rectangle Frame tool	F	F

Rectangle tool	M	M
Ellipse tool	L	L
Rotate tool	R	R
Scale tool	S	S
Shear tool	O	O
Free Transform tool	E	E
Eyedropper tool	I	I
Measure tool	K	K
Gradient tool	G	G
Scissors tool	C	C
Hand tool	H	H
Temporarily selects Hand tool	Spacebar (Layout mode), Alt (Text mode), or Alt+Spacebar (both)	Spacebar (Layout mode), Option (Text mode), or Option+Spacebar (both)
Zoom tool	Z	Z
Temporarily selects Zoom In tool	Ctrl+Spacebar	Command+Spacebar

Toggle Fill and Stroke	X	X
Swap Fill and Stroke	Shift+X	Shift+X
Toggle between Formatting Affects Container and Formatting Affects Text	J	J
Apply Color	, [comma]	, [comma]
Apply Gradient	. [period]	. [period]
Apply No Color	/	/
Switch between Normal View and Preview Mode	W	W
Frame Grid tool (horizontal)	Y	Y
Frame Grid tool (vertical)	Q	Q

Gradient Feather tool	Shift+G	Shift+G

Keys for Selecting and Moving Objects.

This table lists only keyboard shortcuts that aren't displayed in menu commands or tool tips.

Result	Windows Shortcut	Mac OS Shortcut
Temporarily select Selection or Direct Selection tool (last used)	Any tool (except selection tools)+Ctrl	Any tool (except selection tools)+ Command
Temporarily select Group Selection tool	Direct Selection tool+Alt; or Pen, Add Anchor Point, or Delete Anchor Point tool+Alt+Ctrl	Direct Selection tool+Option; or Pen, Add Anchor Point, or Delete Anchor Point tool+Option+Command
Select container of selected content	Esc or double-click	Esc or double-click

Select content of selected container	Shift+Esc or double-click	Shift+Esc or double-click
Add to or subtract from a selection of multiple objects	Selection, Direct Selection, or Group Selection tool+Shift–click (to deselect, click center point)	Selection, Direct Selection, or Group Selection tool+Shift–click (to deselect, click center point)
Duplicate selection	Selection, Direct Selection, or Group Selection tool+Alt–drag*	Selection, Direct Selection, or Group Selection tool+Option–drag*
Duplicate and offset selection	Alt+Left Arrow, Right Arrow, Up Arrow, or Down Arrow key	Option+Left Arrow, Right Arrow, Up Arrow, or Down Arrow key
Duplicate and offset selection by 10 times**	Alt+Shift+Left Arrow, Right Arrow, Up Arrow, Down Arrow key	Option+Shift+Left Arrow, Right Arrow, Up Arrow, Down Arrow key

Move selection**	Left Arrow, Right Arrow, Up Arrow, Down Arrow key	Left Arrow, Right Arrow, Up Arrow, Down Arrow key
Move selection by 10th**	Ctrl+Shift+Left Arrow, Right Arrow, Up Arrow, Down arrow key	Command+Shift+Left Arrow, Right Arrow, Up Arrow, Down arrow key
Move selection by 10 times**	Shift+Left Arrow, Right Arrow, Up Arrow, Down Arrow key	Shift+Left Arrow, Right Arrow, Up Arrow, Down Arrow key
Select master page item from document page	Selection or Direct Selection tool+Ctrl+Shift−click	Selection or Direct Selection tool+Command+Shift−click
Select next object behind or in front	Selection tool+Ctrl−click, or Selection tool+Alt+Ctrl−click	Selection tool+Command−click or Selection tool+Option+Command−click
Select next or previous	Alt+Ctrl+Page Down/ Alt+Ctrl+Page Up	Option+Command+Page Down/ Option+Command+Page Up

frame in story		
Select first or last frame in story	Shift+Alt+Ctrl +Page Down/ Shift+Alt+Ctrl +Page Up	Shift+Option+Comma nd+Page Down/ Shift+Option+Comma nd+Page Up

*Press Shift to constrain movement to 45° angles.

**Amount is set in Edit > Preferences > Units & Increments (Windows) or InDesign > Preferences > Units & Increments (Mac OS).

Keys for Transforming Objects.

This table lists only keyboard shortcuts that aren't displayed in menu commands or tool tips.

Result	Windows Shortcut	Mac OS Shortcut
Duplicate and transform selection	Transformati on tool+Alt– drag*	Transformation tool+Option–drag*
Display Transform tool dialog box	Select object+doubl e-click Scale tool, Rotate tool, or Shear tool in Toolbox	Select object+double-click Scale tool, Rotate tool, or Shear tool in Toolbox

Decrease scale by 1%	Ctrl+,	Command+,
Decrease scale by 5%	Ctrl+Alt+,	Command+Option+,
Increase scale by 1%	Ctrl+.	Command+.
Increase scale by 5%	Ctrl+Alt+.	Command+Option+.
Resize frame and content	Selection tool+Ctrl–drag	Selection tool+Command–drag
Resize frame and content proportionately	Selection tool+Shift+Ctrl–drag	Selection tool+Shift+Command–drag
Constrain proportion	Ellipse tool, Polygon tool, or Rectangle tool+Shift–drag	Ellipse tool, Polygon tool, or Rectangle tool+Shift–drag
Switch image from High Quality Display to Fast Display	Ctrl+Alt+Shift+Z	Command+Option+Shift+Z

*After you select a transformation tool, hold down the mouse button, and then hold down Alt (Windows) or Option (Mac OS) and drag. Press Shift to constrain movement to 45° angles.

Keys for Editing Paths and Frames.

This table lists only keyboard shortcuts that aren't displayed in menu commands or tool tips.

Result	Windows Shortcut	Mac OS Shortcut
Temporarily select Convert Direction Point tool	Direct Selection tool+Alt+Ctrl, or Pen tool+Alt	Direct Selection tool+Option+ Command, or Pen tool+Option
Temporarily switch between Add Anchor Point and Delete Anchor Point tool	Alt	Option
Temporarily select Add Anchor Point tool	Scissors tool+Alt	Scissors tool+Option
Keep Pen tool selected when pointer is over path or anchor point	Pen tool+Shift	Pen tool+Shift
Move anchor point and handles while drawing	Pen tool+spacebar	Pen tool+spacebar
Display the Stroke panel	F10	Command+F10

Keys for Tables.

This table lists only keyboard shortcuts that aren't displayed in menu commands or tool tips.

Result	Windows Shortcut	Mac OS Shortcut
Insert or delete rows or columns while dragging	Begin dragging row or column border, and then hold down Alt as you drag	Begin dragging row or column border, and then hold down Option as you drag
Resize rows or columns without changing the size of the table	Shift–drag interior row or column border	Shift–drag interior row or column border
Resize rows or columns proportionally	Shift–drag right or bottom table border	Shift–drag right or bottom table border
Move to next/previous cell	Tab/Shift+Tab	Tab/Shift+Tab
Move to first/last cell in column	Alt+Page Up/ Alt+Page Down	Option+Page Up/ Option+Page Down
Move to first/last cell in row	Alt+Home/ Alt+End	Option+Home/ Option+End

Move to first/last row in frame	Page Up/Page Down	Page Up/Page Down
Move up/down one cell	Up Arrow/Down Arrow	Up Arrow/Down Arrow
Move left/right one cell	Left Arrow/Right Arrow	Left Arrow/Right Arrow
Select cell above/below the current cell	Shift+Up Arrow/ Shift+Down Arrow	Shift+Up Arrow/ Shift+Down Arrow
Select cell to the right/left of the current cell	Shift+Right Arrow/ Shift+Left Arrow	Shift+Right Arrow/ Shift+Left Arrow
Start row on next column	Enter (numeric keypad)	Enter (numeric keypad)
Start row on next frame	Shift+Enter (numeric keypad)	Shift+Enter (numeric keypad)
Toggle between text selection and cell selection	Esc	Esc

Keys for Finding and Changing Text.

This table lists only keyboard shortcuts that aren't displayed in menu commands or tool tips.

Result	Windows Shortcut	Mac OS Shortcut
Insert selected text into Find What box	Ctrl+F1	Command+F1
Insert selected text into Find What box and finds next	Shift+F1	Shift+F1
Find next occurrence of Find What text	Shift+F2 or Alt+Ctrl+F	Shift+F2 or Option+Command+F
Insert selected text into Change To box	Ctrl+F2	Command+F2
Replace selection with Change To text	Ctrl+F3	Command+F3

Keys for Working with Type.

This table lists only keyboard shortcuts that aren't displayed in menu commands or tool tips.

Result	Windows Shortcut	Mac OS Shortcut
Bold (only for fonts with bold face)	Shift+Ctrl+B	Shift+Command+B
Italic (only for fonts with italic face)	Shift+Ctrl+I	Shift+Command+I
Normal	Shift+Ctrl+Y	Shift+Command+Y
Underline	Shift+Ctrl+U	Shift+Command+U
Strikethrough	Shift+Ctrl+/	Control+Shift+Command+/
All caps (on/off)	Shift+Ctrl+K	Shift+Command+K
Asian language hyphenation	Shift+Ctrl+K	Shift+Command+K
Small caps (on/off)	Shift+Ctrl+H	Shift+Command+H
Tate-chu-yoko setting	Shift+Ctrl+H	Shift+Command+H

Superscri pt	Shift+Ctrl+(+) [plus sign]	Shift+Command+(+) [plus sign]
Subscript	Shift+Alt+Ctrl +(+) [plus sign]	Shift+Option+Comma nd+(+) [plus sign]
Reset horizonta l or vertical scale to 100%	Shift+Ctrl+X or Shift+Alt+Ctrl +X	Shift+Command+X or Shift+Option+Comma nd+X
Basic letter group setting or detail setting	Shift+Ctrl+X or Shift+Alt+Ctrl +X	Shift+Command+X or Shift+Option+Comma nd+X
Align left, right, or center	Shift+Ctrl+L, R, or C	Shift+Command+L, R, or C
Justify all lines	Shift+Ctrl+F (all lines) or J (all but last line)	Shift+Command+F (all lines) or J (all but last line)
Align both ends or equal spacing	Shift+Ctrl+F (align both end) or J (equal spacing)	Shift+Command+F (align both ends) or J (equal spacing)
Increase or decrease	Shift+Ctrl+> or <	Shift+Command+> or <

point size*		
Increase or decrease point size by five times*	Shift+Ctrl+Alt +> or <	Shift+Command+ Option+> or <
Increase or decrease leading (horizont al text)*	Alt+Up Arrow/ Alt+Down Arrow	Option+Up Arrow/ Option+Down Arrow
Increase or decrease leading (vertical text)*	Alt+Right Arrow/ Alt+Left Arrow	Option+Right Arrow/ Option+Left Arrow
Increase or decrease leading by five times (horizont al text)*	Alt+Ctrl+Up Arrow/ Alt+Ctrl+Down Arrow	Option+Command+U p Arrow/ Option+Command+D own Arrow
Increase or decrease	Alt+Ctrl+Right Arrow/	Option+Command+Ri ght Arrow/

leading by five times (vertical text)*	Alt+Ctrl+Left Arrow	Option+Command+Left Arrow
Auto leading	Shift+Alt+Ctrl +A	Shift+Option+Command+A
Align to grid (on/off)	Shift+Alt+Ctrl +G	Shift+Option+Command+G
Auto-hyphenate (on/off)	Shift+Alt+Ctrl +H	Shift+Option+Command+H
Increase or decrease kerning and tracking (horizontal text)	Alt+Left Arrow/Alt+Right Arrow	Option+Left Arrow/ Option+Right Arrow
Increase or decrease kerning and tracking (vertical text)	Alt+Up Arrow/ Alt+Down Arrow	Option+Up Arrow/ Option+Down Arrow
Increase or	Alt+Ctrl+Left Arrow/	Option+Command+Left Arrow/

decrease kerning and tracking by five times (horizontal text)	Alt+Ctrl+Right Arrow	Option+Command+Right Arrow
Increase or decrease kerning and tracking by five times (vertical text)	Alt+Ctrl+Up Arrow/ Alt+Ctrl+Down Arrow	Option+Command+Up Arrow/ Option+Command+Down Arrow
Increase kerning between words*	Alt+Ctrl+\	Option+Command+\
Decrease kerning between words*	Alt+Ctrl+Backspace	Option+Command+Delete
Clear all manual kerning and reset	Alt+Ctrl+Q	Option+Command+Q

tracking to 0		
Increase or decrease baseline shift** (horizontal text)	Shift+Alt+Up Arrow/ Shift+Alt+Down Arrow	Shift+Option+Up Arrow/ hift+Option+Down Arrow
Increase or decrease baseline shift** (vertical text)	Shift+Alt+Right Arrow/ Shift+Alt+Left Arrow	Shift+Option+Right Arrow/ Shift+Option+Left Arrow
Increase or decrease baseline shift by five times (horizontal text)	Shift+Alt+Ctrl +Up Arrow/ Shift+Alt+Ctrl +Down Arrow	Shift+Option+Comma nd+Up Arrow/ Shift+Option+Comma nd+Down Arrow
Increase or decrease baseline shift by five times	Shift+Alt+Ctrl +Right Arrow/ Shift+Alt+Ctrl +Left Arrow	Shift+Option+Comma nd+Right Arrow/ hift+Option+Comman d+Left Arrow

(vertical text)		
Automatically flow story	Shift–click loaded text icon	Shift–click loaded text icon
Semi-automatically flow story	Alt–click loaded text icon	Option–click loaded text icon
Recompose all stories	Alt+Ctrl+/	Option+Command+/
Insert current page number	Alt+Ctrl+N	Option+Command+N

*Press Shift to increase or decrease kerning between words by five times.

**Amount is set in Edit > Preferences > Units & Increments (Windows) or InDesign > Preferences > Units & Increments (Mac OS).

Keys for Navigating Through and Selecting Text.

This table lists only shortcuts that aren't displayed in menu commands or tool tips.

Result	Windows Shortcut	Mac OS Shortcut
Move to right or left one character	Right Arrow/ Left Arrow	Right Arrow/ Left Arrow
Move up or down one line	Up Arrow/ Down Arrow	Up Arrow/ Down Arrow
Move to right or left one word	Ctrl+Right Arrow/ Ctrl+Left Arrow	Command+Right Arrow/ Command+Left Arrow
Move to start or end of line	Home/End	Home/End
Move to previous or next paragraph	Ctrl+Up Arrow/ Ctrl+Down Arrow	Command+Up Arrow/ Command+Down Arrow
Move to start or end of story	Ctrl+Home/ Ctrl+End	Command+Home/ Command+End
Select one word	Double-click word	Double-click word
Select one character right or left	Shift+Right Arrow/ Shift+Left Arrow	Shift+Right Arrow/ Shift+Left Arrow

Select one line above or below	Shift+Up Arrow/ Shift+Down Arrow	Shift+Up Arrow/ Shift+Down Arrow
Select start or end of line	Shift+Home/ Shift+End	Shift+Home/ Shift+End
Select one paragraph	Triple-click or quadruple-click paragraph, depending on Text Preferences setting	Triple-click or quadruple-click paragraph, depending on Text Preferences setting
Select one paragraph before or after	Shift+Ctrl+Up Arrow/ Shift+Ctrl+Down Arrow	Shift+Command+Up Arrow/ Shift+Command+Down Arrow
Select current line	Shift+Ctrl+\	Shift+Command+\
Select characters from insertion point	Shift–click	Shift–click
Select start or end of story	Shift+Ctrl+Home/ Shift+Ctrl+End	Shift+Command+Home/ Shift+Command+End

Select all in story	Ctrl+A	Command+A
Select first/last frame	Shift+Alt+Ctrl+Page Up/ Shift+Alt+Ctrl+Page Down	Shift+Option+Command+Page Up/ Shift+Option+Command+Page Down
Select previous/ next frame	Alt+Ctrl+Page Up/ Alt+Ctrl+Page Down	Option+Command+Page Up/ Option+Command+Page Down
Delete word in front of insertion point (Story Editor)	Ctrl+Backspace or Delete	Command+Delete or Del (numeric keypad)
Update missing font list	Ctrl+Alt+Shift+/	Command+Option+Shift+/

Keys for viewing documents and document workspaces.

This table lists only shortcuts that aren't displayed in menu commands or tool tips.

Result	Windows Shortcut	Mac OS Shortcut
Temporarily select Hand tool	Spacebar (with no text insertion point), Alt-drag (with text insertion point), or Alt+spacebar (in both text and non-text modes)	Spacebar (with no text insertion point), Option–drag (with text insertion point), or Option+spacebar (in both text and nontext modes)
Temporarily select Zoom In tool	Ctrl+spacebar	Command+spacebar
Temporarily select Zoom Out tool	Alt+Ctrl+spacebar or Alt+Zoom In tool	Option+Command+spacebar or Option+Zoom In tool
Zoom to 50%, 200%, or 400%	Ctrl+5, 2, or 4	Command+5, 2, or 4
Redraw screen	Shift+F5	Shift+F5
Open new default document	Ctrl+Alt+N	Command+Option+N

Switch between current and previous zoom levels	Alt+Ctrl+2	Option+Command+2
Switch to next/previous document window	Ctrl+~ [tilde]/ Shift+Ctrl+F6 or Ctrl+Shift+~ [tilde]	Command+F6 or Command+~ [tilde]/ Command+Shift+~ [tilde]
Scroll up/down one screen	Page Up/Page Down	Page Up/Page Down
Go back/forward to last-viewed page	Ctrl+Page Up/ Ctrl+Page Down	Command+Page Up/ Command+Page Down
Go to previous/next spread	Alt+Page Up/ Alt+Page Down	Option+Page Up/ Option+Page Down
Fit spread in window	Double-click Hand tool	Double-click Hand tool
Activate the Go To command	Ctrl+J	Command+J
Fit selection in window	Ctrl+Alt+(+) [plus sign]	Command+Option+(+) [plus sign]

Display the entire object	Ctrl+Alt+(+) [plus sign]	Command+Option+(+) [plus sign]
Go to master page while \ panel is closed	Ctrl+J, type prefix of master, press Enter	Command+J, type prefix of master, press Return
Cycle through units of measurement	Shift+Alt+Ctrl +U	Shift+Option+Command+U
Snap guide to ruler increments	Shift–drag guide	Shift–drag guide
Switch between page and spread guides (creation only)	Ctrl–drag guide	Command–drag guide
Temporarily turn on/off snap to		Control-drag object
Create vertical and	Ctrl–drag from zero point	Command–drag from zero point

horizontal ruler guides for the spread		
Select all guides	Alt+Ctrl+G	Option+Command+G
Lock or unlock zero point	Right-click zero point and choose an option	Control–click zero point and choose an option
Use current magnificati on for view threshold of new guide	Alt–drag guide	Option–drag guide
Select buttons in alert dialog boxes	Press first letter of button name, if underlined	Press first letter of button name
Show informatio n on installed plug-ins and InDesign component s	Ctrl+Help > About Design	Command+InDesign menu > About InDesign

Keys for Working with XML.

This table lists only shortcuts that aren't displayed in menu commands or tool tips.

Result	Windows Shortcut	Mac OS Shortcut
Expand/Collapse element	Right Arrow/Left Arrow	Right Arrow/Left Arrow
Expand/Collapse element and child elements	Alt+Right Arrow/ Alt+Left Arrow	Option+Right Arrow/ Option+Left Arrow
Extend XML selection up/down	Shift+Up Arrow/ Shift+Down Arrow	Shift+Up Arrow/ Shift+Down Arrow
Move XML selection up/down	Up Arrow/ Down Arrow	Up Arrow/ Down Arrow
Scroll structure pane up/down one screen	Page Up/ Page Down	Page Up/ Page Down
Select first/last XML node	Home/ End	Home/ End
Extend selection to	Shift+Home/ Shift+End	Shift+Home/ Shift+End

first/last XML node		
Go to previous/next validation error	Ctrl+Left Arrow/ Ctrl+Right Arrow	Command+Left Arrow/ Command+Right Arrow
Automatically tag text frames and tables	Ctrl+Alt+Shift+F7	Command+Option+Shift+F7

Keys for Indexing.

This table lists only shortcuts that aren't displayed in menu commands or tool tips.

Result	Windows Shortcut	Mac OS Shortcut
Create index entry without dialog box (alphanumeric only)	Shift+Ctrl+Alt+[	Shift+Command+Option+[
Open index entry dialog box	Ctrl+7	Command+7
Create proper	Shift+Ctrl+Alt+]	Shift+Command+Option+]

name index entry (last name, first name)		

Keys for Panels.

This table lists only shortcuts that aren't displayed in menu commands or tool tips.

Result	Windows Shortcut	Mac OS Shortcut
Delete without confirmation	Alt-click Delete icon	Option-click Delete icon
Create item and set options	Alt-click New button	Option-click New button
Apply value and keep focus on option	Shift+Enter	Shift+Enter
Activate last-used option in last-used panel	Ctrl+Alt+~ [tilde]	Command+Option+~ [tilde]
Select range of styles,	Shift-click	Shift-click

layers, links, swatches, or library objects in a panel		
Select nonadjacent styles, layers, links, swatches, or library objects in a panel	Ctrl-click	Command-click
Apply value and select next value	Tab	Tab
Move focus to selected object, text, or window	Esc	Esc
Show/Hide all panels, Toolbox, and Control panel (with no insertion point)	Tab	Tab
Show/Hide all panels except the Toolbox and	Shift+Tab	Shift+Tab

Control panel (docked or not)		
Open or close all stashed panels	Ctrl+Alt+Tab	Command+Option+Tab
Stash a panel group	Alt+drag any panel tab (in the group) to edge of screen	Option+drag any panel tab (in the group) to edge of window
Select item by name	Alt+Ctrl-click in list, and then use keyboard to select item by name	Option+Command-click in list and then use keyboard to select item by name
Open the Drop Shadow panel	Alt+Ctrl+M	Command+Option+M

Keys for the Control Panel.

This table lists only shortcuts that aren't displayed in menu commands or tool tips.

Result	Windows Shortcut	Mac OS Shortcut
Toggle focus to/from Control panel	Ctrl+6	Command+6
Toggle Character/Paragraph text attributes mode	Ctrl+Alt+7	Command+Option+7
Change reference point when proxy has focus	Any key on the numeric keypad or keyboard numbers	Any key on the numeric keypad or keyboard numbers
Display the pop-up menu that has focus	Alt+Down Arrow	
Open Units & Increments Preferences	Alt-click Kerning icon	Option-click Kerning icon
Open the Text Frame Options dialog box	Alt-click Number Of Columns icon	Option-click Number of Columns icon
Open the Move dialog box	Alt-click X or Y icon	Option-click X or Y icon
Open the Rotate dialog box	Alt-click Angle icon	Option-click Angle icon
Open the Scale dialog box	Alt-click X or Y Scale icon	Option-click X or Y Scale icon

Open the Shear dialog box	Alt-click Shear icon	Option-click Shear icon
Open Text Preferences	Alt-click Superscript, Subscript, or Small Caps button	Option-click Superscript, Subscript, or Small Caps button
Open the Underline Options dialog box	Alt-click Underline button	Option-click Underline button
Open the Strikethrough Options dialog box	Alt-click Strikethrough button	Option-click Strikethrough button
Open the Grids Preferences	Alt-click Align To Baseline Grid, or Do Not Align To Baseline Grid button	Option-click Align To Baseline Grid, or Do Not Align To Baseline Grid button
Open the Drop Caps & Nested Styles dialog box	Alt-click Drop Cap Number Of Lines, or Drop Cap One Or More Characters icon	Option-click Drop Cap Number Of Lines, or Drop Cap One Or More Characters icon

Open the Justification dialog box	Alt-click Leading icon	Option-click Leading icon
Open Named Grid dialog box	Double-click Named Grid icon	Double-click Named Grid icon
Open New Named Grid Options dialog box	Alt-click Named Grid icon	Option-click Named Grid icon
Open Frame Grid Options dialog box	Alt-click Number of characters Horizontal, Number of Characters Vertical, Character Aki, Line Aki, Vertical Scale, Horizontal Scale, Grid View, Font Size, Number of Columns, or Column Gutter icon	Option-click Number of characters Horizontal, Number of Characters Vertical, Character Aki, Line Aki, Vertical Scale, Horizontal Scale, Grid View, Font Size, Number of Columns, or Column Gutter icon

Keys for Type Panels and Dialog Boxes.

This table isn't a complete list of keyboard shortcuts. It lists only those shortcuts that aren't displayed in menu commands or tool tips.

Result	Windows Shortcut	Mac OS Shortcut
Open Justification dialog box	Alt+Ctrl+Shift+J	Option+Command+Shift+J
Open Paragraph Rules dialog box	Alt+Ctrl+J	Option+Command+J
Open Keep Options dialog box	Alt+Ctrl+K	Option+Command+K
Activate Character panel	Ctrl+T	Command+T
Activate Paragraph panel	Ctrl+Alt+T	Command+Option+T

Keys for the Character and Paragraph Styles.

This table lists only shortcuts that aren't displayed in menu commands or tool tips.

Result	Windows Shortcut	Mac OS Shortcut
Make character style definition match text	Select text and press Shift+Alt+Ctrl+C	Select text and press Shift+Option+Command+C
Make paragraph style definition match text	Select text and press Shift+Alt+Ctrl+R	Select text and press Shift+Option+Command+R
Change options without applying style	Shift+Alt+Ctrl-double-click style	Shift+Option+Command-double-click style
Remove style and local formatting	Alt-click paragraph style name	Option-click paragraph style name
Clear overrides from	Alt+Shift-click paragraph style name	Option+Shift-click paragraph style name

paragrap h style		
Show/hid e Paragrap h and Character Styles panels, respectiv ely	F11, Shift+F11	Command+F11, Command+Shift+F11

Keys for the Tabs Panel.

This table lists only shortcuts that aren't displayed in menu commands or tool tips.

Result	Windows Shortcut	Mac OS Shortcut
Activate Tabs panel	Shift+Ctrl+T	Shift+Command+T
Switch between alignment options	Alt-click tab	Option-click tab

Keys for the Layers Panel.

This table lists only shortcuts that aren't displayed in menu commands or tool tips.

Result	Windows Shortcut	Mac OS Shortcut
Select all objects on layer	Alt-click layer	Option-click layer
Copy selection to new layer	Alt-drag small square to new layer	Option-drag small square to new layer
Add new layer below selected layer	Ctrl-click Create New Layer	Command-click Create New Layer
Add new layer to the top of the layer list	Shift+Ctrl-click Create New Layer	Shift+Command-click Create New Layer
Add new layer to the top of the layer list and open New Layer dialog box	Shift+Alt+Ctrl-click Create New Layer	Cmd+Option+Shift-click Create New Layer
Add new layer and open New Layer dialog box	Alt-click Create New Layer	Option-click Create New Layer

Keys for the Pages Panel.

This table lists only shortcuts that aren't displayed in menu commands or tool tips.

Result	Windows Shortcut	Mac OS Shortcut
Apply master to selected page	Alt-click master	Option-click master
Base another master page on selected master	Alt-click the master you want to base the selected master on	Option-click the master you want to base the selected master on
Create master page	Ctrl-click Create New Page button	Command-click Create New Page button
Display Insert Pages dialog box	Alt-click New Page button	Option-click New Page button
Add new page after last page	Shift+Ctrl+P	Shift+Command+P

Keys for the Color Panel.

This table lists only shortcuts that aren't displayed in menu commands or tool tips.

Result	Windows Shortcut	Mac OS Shortcut
Move color sliders in tandem	Shift-drag slider	Shift-drag slider
Select a color for the nonactive fill or stroke	Alt-click color bar	Option-click color bar
Switch between color modes (CMYK, RGB, LAB)	Shift-click color bar	Shift-click color bar

Keys for using the Separations Preview Panel.

This table lists only shortcuts that aren't displayed in menu commands or tool tips.

Result	Windows Shortcut	Mac OS Shortcut
Turn on Overprint preview	Ctrl+Alt+Shift+Y	Command+Option+Shift+Y

Show all plates	Ctrl+Alt+Shift +~ [tilde]	Command+Option+Shift+~ [tilde]
Show Cyan plate	Ctrl+Alt+Shift +1	Command+Option+Shift+1
Show Magent a plate	Ctrl+Alt+Shift +2	Command+Option+Shift+2
Show Yellow plate	Ctrl+Alt+Shift +3	Command+Option+Shift+3
Show Black plate	Ctrl+Alt+Shift +4	Command+Option+Shift+4
Show 1st Spot plate	Ctrl+Alt+Shift +5	Command+Option+Shift+5
Show 2nd Spot plate	Ctrl+Alt+Shift +6	Command+Option+Shift+6
Show 3rd Spot plate	Ctrl+Alt+Shift +7	Command+Option+Shift+7

Keys for the Swatches Panel.

This table lists only shortcuts that aren't displayed in menu commands or tool tips.

Result	Windows Shortcut	Mac OS Shortcut
Create new swatch based on the current swatch	Alt-click New Swatch button	Option-click New Swatch button
Create spot color swatch based on the current swatch	Alt+Ctrl-click New Swatch button	Option+Command-click New Swatch button
Change options without applying swatch	Shift+Alt+Ctrl -double-click swatch	Shift+Option+Command -double-click swatch

Keys for the Transform Panel.

This table lists only shortcuts that aren't displayed in menu commands or tool tips.

Result	Windows Shortcut	Mac OS Shortcut
Apply value and copy object	Alt+Enter	Option+Enter
Apply width, height, or scale value proportionally	Ctrl+Enter	Command+Enter

Keys for Resolving Conflicts between Mac OS 10.3x and 10.4

This table lists only shortcuts that aren't displayed in menu commands or tool tips.

Result	Mac OS Shortcut
Open Preferences dialog box	Command+K
Open Paragraph Styles panel	Command+F11
Open Character Styles panel	Command+Shift+F11
Open Swatches panel	F5
Open Pages panel	Command+F12
Minimize active application window	Command+M
Hide application	Command+H

Applies to: *Adobe InDesign.*

Customer's Page.

This page is for customers who enjoyed Adobe InDesign Keyboard Shortcuts.

Our beloved and respectable reader, we thank you very much for your patronage. Please we will appreciate it more if you rate and review this book; that is if it was helpful to you. Thank you.

Download Our EBooks Today For Free.

In order to appreciate our customers, we have made some of our titles available at 0.00. They are totally free. Feel free to get a copy of the free titles.

Here are books we give to our customers free of charge:

(A) For Keyboard Shortcuts in Windows check:

Windows 7 Keyboard Shortcuts.

(B) For Keyboard Shortcuts in Office 2016 for Windows check:

Word 2016 Keyboard Shortcuts For Windows.

(C) For Keyboard Shortcuts in Office 2016 for Mac check:

OneNote 2016 Keyboard Shortcuts For Macintosh.

Follow this link to download any of the titles listed above for free.

Note: Feel free to download them from our website or your favorite bookstore today. Thank you.

Other Books By This Publisher.

Titles for single programs under Shortcut Matters Series are not part of this list.

S/N	Title	Series
Series A: Limits Breaking Quotes.		
1	Discover Your Key Christian Quotes	Limits Breaking Quotes
Series B: Shortcut Matters.		
1	Windows 7 Shortcuts	Shortcut Matters
2	Windows 7 Shortcuts & Tips	Shortcut Matters
3	Windows 8.1 Shortcuts	Shortcut Matters
4	Windows 10 Shortcut Keys	Shortcut Matters
5	Microsoft Office 2007 Keyboard Shortcuts For Windows.	Shortcut Matters
6	Microsoft Office 2010 Shortcuts For Windows.	Shortcut Matters
7	Microsoft Office 2013 Shortcuts For Windows.	Shortcut Matters
8	Microsoft Office 2016 Shortcuts For Windows.	Shortcut Matters
9	Microsoft Office 2016 Keyboard Shortcuts For Macintosh.	Shortcut Matters
10	Top 11 Adobe Programs Keyboard Shortcuts	Shortcut Matters
11	Top 10 Email Service Providers Keyboard Shortcuts	Shortcut Matters
12	Hot Corel Programs Keyboard Shortcuts	Shortcut Matters

13	Top 10 Browsers Keyboard Shortcuts	Shortcut Matters
14	Microsoft Browsers Keyboard Shortcuts.	Shortcut Matters
15	Popular Email Service Providers Keyboard Shortcuts	Shortcut Matters
16	Professional Video Editing with Keyboard Shortcuts.	Shortcut Matters
17	Popular Web Browsers Keyboard Shortcuts.	Shortcut Matters

Series C: Teach Yourself.

1	Teach Yourself Computer Fundamentals	Teach Yourself
2	Teach Yourself Computer Fundamentals Workbook	Teach Yourself

Series D: For Painless Publishing

1	Self-Publish it with CreateSpace.	For Painless Publishing
2	Where is my money? Now solved for Kindle and CreateSpace	For Painless Publishing
3	Describe it on Amazon	For Painless Publishing

63244134R00046

Made in the USA
Lexington, KY
01 May 2017